Creative Movement for Special Education

A Guide to Activities Throughout the School Year

Sharen Metz Kokaska

Fearon Publishers, Inc.
Belmont, California

Designed by Jane Mitchell
Illustrated by Marty Viljamaa

Copyright © MCMLXXIV by Fearon Publishers, Inc., 6 Davis Drive, Belmont, California 94002. Member of the Pitman Group. All rights reserved. No part of this book may be reproduced by any means, transmitted, or translated into a machine language without written permission from the publisher.

ISBN-0-8224-1662-X

Library of Congress Catalog Card Number: 74-81747

Printed in the United States of America.

Contents

Acknowledgments   iv
Preface   v
Introduction   1
Back to School: A New Approach   7
The Fall Season: A Time of Change   12
Halloween: Fun and Fantasy   18
Thanksgiving: Past and Present   26
Christmas and Hanukkah: Celebrating Together   32
The Winter Season: Snow Play and Seclusion   38
Three Special Days: People to Remember   43
The Spring Season: A Time of Splendor   48
Easter: Animals and Amusements   53
The Summer Season: Recreational Pursuits   59
Bibliography   65

Acknowledgments

My personal thanks is extended to Lois Johnson, who directed the workshop in which I discovered the field of movement education. Through her program I became acquainted with the various approaches to movement and found my home in creative expression.

Gratitude is also extended to my principal, Fred London, who encouraged my work and allowed me to experiment with the special curriculum. Recognition goes to the children who willingly acted upon my ideas and unselfishly provided many of their own.

Special thanks goes to my husband, Chuck, who is a source of continuing assistance and support in my educational endeavors.

Preface

The exceptional child is one who often experiences failure, discouragement, and frustration in his daily activities. He competes in a society which places strong emphasis upon academic performance and success, yet he must face these challenges knowing that he lacks many of the skills necessary for achievement. Special classes and tutorial assistance have changed this situation by providing for individualized instruction within a positive learning environment. By working at his own rate, each child gains the knowledge and skills which can help him to become a productive member of society. However, academic accomplishment is only one part of a total program in special education.

The exceptional child also needs to experience success in his physical surroundings. He frequently suffers from inadequate spatial awareness, lack of body image, and limited coordination. As he moves within the regular school environment, he is constantly confronted with his physical inadequacies. Many physical education programs have attempted to remedy the situation through specialized training, particularly in the perceptual-motor area. More recently, the field of movement exploration has offered children a means of improving skills without worrisome competition or fear of failure. In the race to improve performance, however, creative experiences have been sorely neglected.

Creative movement should be included in every special education program. It offers the exceptional child an opportunity to explore space, improve body image, and gain coordination in a relaxed atmosphere. It is similar to movement exploration in that both are child centered, informal, and noncompetitive. Creative experiences stress movement for self-expression rather than for problem solving. By concentrating on himself, the child discovers he can move in many different ways. Success and security in these movements pave the way for further development of other physical skills.

Creative Movement for Special Education represents a collection of ideas utilized with retarded and slow-learning children at the Silver Spur Elementary School in Palos Verdes, California. The lessons were created for a functional curriculum in which concrete experiences formed the basis for learning. Movement was a medium through which children identified with themes and increased their understanding of themselves and the environment. Creative movement also freed the children's imaginations, allowing them to become a part of nature, animate beings, or fantasy characters. For some, it became a whole new way of experiencing life.

Sharen Metz Kokaska

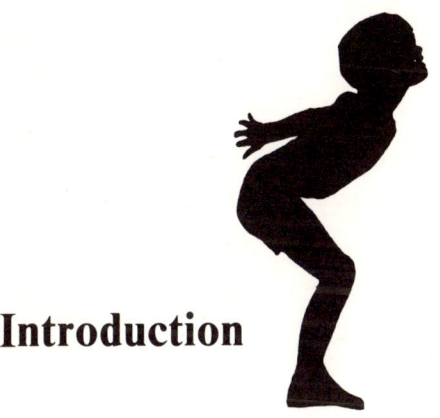

Introduction

    Creative movement is an approach to learning that emphasizes self-expression through sensory-motor experiences. Children are presented with an idea, poem, or story upon which they improvise movement, often to musical accompaniment. Themes can originate either with the teacher or with the participants who design their own variations as the activity is in progress. Perceptual awareness is a natural consequence of movement as children interpret and express motion in a unique, personal manner.

    Creative movement is most frequently utilized with the young child, but can have equal significance for children of all ages. The activities in this book are oriented toward the exceptional child who often has difficulty expressing himself. Movement experience offers these children a medium for self-expression that is acceptable at all levels. Responses can range from the limited to the elaborate, as each child becomes involved in his own interpretation of themes. Restricted speech and intelligence are accomodated by this approach, because the child's body, not his language, is the spokesman for self-expression.

    Creative movement provides all children with an opportunity to experiment with ideas, display emotions, and improvise actions within a well-defined framework. In addition, it allows for exploration and assimilation of new information in a personalized manner. Moving creatively is an enjoyable method for experiencing one's self within the environment.

Objectives

The objectives of creative movement for exceptional children reflect those of the special curriculum: involvement, significance, and success. These goals form the basis for remediation in all subject areas. Together, they pave the way for a meaningful program in which transfer of learning can take place.

Involvement. Involvement is necessary if material is to have significance for children, particularly those who have difficulty conceptualizing and/or expressing themselves. The process of involvement is relatively simple to explain. As a child becomes concerned with his own movements, he begins to make a physical statement about himself. The more he can express upon a given theme, the more he will reveal. By interacting with the theme, he gains understanding of his body motions and the subject matter. For example, if a child pretends to be a falling leaf, he considers his knowledge about a leaf and then translates that knowledge into movement. Meanwhile, he must also make a basic decision about the degree of freedom he is willing to experience. By testing such parameters, the child acquires information about his own movements as well as those of the object he imitates.

In terms of behavioral objectives, involvement cannot be measured by a standardized test. However, it can be charted for an individual child in terms of:

1. The time he devotes to creative movement (ten minutes one day, fifteen minutes the next).
2. The number of alternative suggestions he provides ("I can do it like this or this").
3. The amount of imitation versus creativity he displays in a given lesson (child investigates more of his own movements than those of others).
4. The verbal reflections he provides on a task ("I really felt like a tree").
5. The amount of independence he displays in a lesson (child seeks less direction from the teacher).

These criteria can be used by the teacher to observe changes in an individual's performance over a period of time.

Significance. Creative movement is a significant reinforcer of learning concepts. The approach is somewhat similar to "learning by doing," because movement requires physical involvement of the participants. In other words, when an individual acts upon a theme, it becomes personally significant to him. The information he gains from such experiences is then incorporated into his memory for future use. Recall is easier if the child has actually participated in an exercise on that topic. For example, the process of transformation from caterpillar to butterfly is more easily recalled by children who have acted out the various stages of development than by those who have not. Holidays, historical events, famous people, and changes in nature can become more meaningful to the learner if he engages in related movement activities. Furthermore, the material becomes a natural extension of himself, if the child has the opportunity to incorporate it through his own, personal actions.

Success. In a creative approach, every child who designs movement on his own can experience success. All responses to a theme are accepted because there are no right or wrong answers. The teacher's role is to guide children in their interpretation of themes by suggesting variations or techniques. "How would it feel to be a snowflake?" is a question all children can answer with their bodies. Encouragement to "be light and airy" is one approach to try with the hesitant child.

Exceptional children are often unsure of themselves and may imitate peers during the first few lessons of movement. Reassurance from the teacher to "do it your own way" can lend the support that is needed to encourage children to experiment by themselves. Those few who will not willingly create on their own can profit from observation and imitation in initial exercises.

The teacher must be careful to avoid criticizing children's movements, as she may discourage certain forms of creative expression. It is sometimes helpful to suggest an alternative method of action for those who are having difficulty interpreting the theme. For example, if a child is portraying a scarecrow as rigid rather than floppy, the teacher might suggest he try relaxing one part of his body at a time, until he becomes very limp. When this information is transferred into self-expression, then personal success becomes a reality.

Preparation

Prior to initiating a program in creative movement, the teacher should consider the following factors: supplementary materials, conditions, and organization.

Supplementary Materials. Although the movement activities may be used in isolation, they are far more effective when combined with other resources. Additional supplies will be necessary if the instructor decides to incorporate movement into a unit of study. Audiovisual equipment, pictures, books, displays, and bulletin boards are a few of the items that can be used. A record player and a variety of records will enhance experiences in the classroom. Selection of music is at the teacher's discretion, as she may want to blend music with other resources.

Before she begins a unit, the teacher should collect films, filmstrips, or film loops and records on that topic. These materials are helpful in explaining to children the events that take place at that time of year. Films establish a setting for self-expression through appropriate coloring and scenery, and music adds to the dramatics through rhythm and tone.

The instructor should also utilize storybooks and pictures to challenge imaginations. Children enjoy fantasy as a prelude to activity and the material is an excellent source of involvement. A short story on fall can depict in words what the children will illustrate in movement. Classroom displays—a leaf collection, for example—add to the atmosphere and encourage children to discover and compare the real world to that of fantasy. Bulletin boards decorated with suitable pictures contribute to the learning environment.

Simple props, such as hats, necklaces, scarves, and rhythm instruments, may be used to accompany movement, and children could construct other useful articles during their art lessons. The teacher should have a drum, tamborine, bells, and sticks at her disposal.

Conditions. Whether or not a teacher uses a unit approach, several conditions must be considered when planning for movement activities. The most important variable is space. A large, empty room, such as a cafeteria or auditorium is preferable. However, the teacher may also use the regular classroom if space is sufficient to allow free, unobstructed movement. A minimum of 4 square feet per child is required for most activities. A bare floor is more desirable than a rug because children like to remove their shoes and socks. Bare feet add to the ease of performance and help to create a feeling of freedom.

The standard procedure is to ask the children to scatter within a designated area after the directions have been given. This way, individuals move about the room or in their own personal space without touching each other. At times, a circle formation is utilized, in which case all children should be visible from the teacher's position.

Organization. A third consideration is the organization of time, materials, and lessons. First, the instructor should decide how much time per week is to be spent on creative movement. Forty-five minutes to an hour is recommended for a single session, although it is possible to start with shorter lessons and gradually extend them. Classes should be held at least once a week, preferably at a regular time in the schedule. Such organization assists the teacher in her planning and provides for continuity in the children's daily routine.

Next, it is important to arrange supplementary materials and/or props so that they are readily accessible. A closet or shelf can be used for easy storage of small items. Larger audiovisual equipment should be ordered as needed, but always assembled before the activities begin.

Selection of supplies becomes an integral part of preparation, especially as it relates to program objectives. It is the teacher's responsibility to decide which items will precede a lesson and what function they will serve. She must be careful to coordinate her choice of materials with the purpose of a given lesson. For example, if the children are to imitate the motions of penguins and walruses, then a film loop on arctic animals would be an appropriate method of demonstrating these actions. On the other hand, the film loop would not be as suitable if the objective were to interpret a poem about penguins and walruses. In this case, it would be better to look at pictures of the animals and discuss their characteristics with the class.

The teacher's final concern should be with the flow of movement in a single session. Generally speaking, a lesson should consist of a prelude, exercise, and summation. The introduction may be presented through a story, picture, film, record, or any other supplementary item. Its purpose is to recall information, stimulate imagination, and set the tone for performance. The teacher then proceeds into directions or suggestions for creative expression as outlined in the following chapters.

Exercise incorporates one or more of the suggested chapter activities into action. Most exercises are open-ended in that additions or changes can be made to suit the needs of the group. Segments within a chapter may be used in any order or combination to produce an effective lesson. The teacher should also be sensitive to suggestions for elaboration from the children. Spontaneity often results in exciting, creative movement, so experiences should be free enough to allow for self-initiated variations.

At the end of a session, the teacher briefly describes and compliments the children on their movements and asks for their reactions. No one is required to comment, but all should feel free to verbalize "what happened" and "how it felt." Summation provides an opportunity to associate the introduction with the exercise and, hence, reinforce learning concepts. A short discussion also allows time for children to reflect upon themselves and their own movements: "I wouldn't want to be a snowman," or "I felt drippy all over." This is a time for synthesizing involvement and success, a time for expressing that which is significant to the individual child.

How to Begin

The activities in this book are arranged in sequence as a guide to creative movement throughout the school year. Begin with the chapter "Back to School." Here, movements are more structured than in later units. The activities in this first chapter are designed to help the children and the teacher become acquainted with the process of creating and "doing your own thing" in a group setting. Many of the exercises call for a circle formation, which lends a certain element of control to these initial experiences. Lessons such as "The Name Game," "Drum Beat," and "This is my Body" are based upon the Orff (1950) technique of rhythm through language. They are oriented toward involvement through repetition, but also allow for individual creativity.

Tell the class that this is "movement time"—a time when they use their bodies to move and their minds to think about what is happening. This simple objective helps children to realize what is expected of them. Some rules of conduct are also necessary to promote harmony within the room. A few basic standards are sufficient for control, yet allow for freedom of response:

1. A signal for attention, such as a bell or drumbeat means to stop, look, and listen.
2. Children move in their own space, even if they "carry" it with them about the room. They should never disturb someone else's space.
3. A child need not participate immediately—he may choose to watch instead—but he is always asked to join the group later on.
4. Any child who interferes with the movement of others is told to sit down for a certain period of time.

These basic rules may be all that is necessary to help the children perform at their best. Basically, an atmosphere of enthusiasm and trust is most conducive to creative expression. When children feel secure in movement and are free to invent, then self-expression is at an optimum.

Back to School:
A New Approach

The opening exercises are oriented toward three general skills: (1) getting acquainted, (2) listening for directions, and (3) demonstrating body image. These items are of major importance during the first few weeks of school, because they influence classroom harmony and the freedom for individual expression.

Children need to feel comfortable in a group in order to concentrate on a given direction, and they must also feel comfortable with themselves in order to demonstrate knowledge about their bodies. Assurance can be gained through interaction with others in an orderly environment. These initial exercises have been organized so that the group works together in a controlled setting. Participation is limited to short, simple responses, and motor involvement is an inherent part of all the activities.

As the class becomes familiar with creative expression, the teacher should note behavior for the specified areas. Are the children learning each other's names? Do they comprehend instructions? In what ways do they exhibit freedom or inhibition of movement? It is also wise to note individual problems with following directions and identification of body parts, as they receive continued emphasis throughout the book.

After a time, the first goal—getting acquainted—will have been attained. However, it is imperative for the teacher to understand that none of the skills need to be perfected in order to progress to the next chapter. For example, all children need not develop an appropriate body image at this time. It is more important for the group to enjoy the activities and, in so doing, demonstrate an ability to work together. As the year progresses the teacher can then chart their progress in the second and third areas.

The Name Game
Formation: Seated in a circle

As the rhyme is spoken, everyone draws a circle in the air with his finger. At the end of each verse, the teacher points to a child, who then demonstrates another way of making a circle. All the children imitate the action and repeat the child's name in rhythm four times.

> Around, around, around is the game
> Around the circle is to know your name.

> *Examples:* Tri-cia, Tri-cia, Tri-cia, Tri-cia; or Co-ri-na, Co-ri-na, Co-ri-na, Co-ri-na.

Drum Beat
Formation: Seated in a circle

Each person's first name is beat in rhythm on the drum and spoken slowly several times. Children count the number of beats in a name and "listen" for their own.

> *Examples:* Da'-vid   Da'-vid   Da'-vid (two beats); or Fran-ches'-ca   Fran-ches'-ca   Fran-ches'-ca (three beats).

> *Variations:* Listen to the beat without verbalizing and guess whose name it is. Listen for the difference in accent on similar names, as "Miss-us   Bag'-da-sar" and "Miss-us   Ko-kas'-ka."

Where is Everybody?
Formation: Scattered about the room
Tune: "Where is Thumbkin?"

As the song is sung, all children hide behind their chairs until a name is called. The designated child then stands up and answers the teacher with the second line of the song. On the last line the child returns to his hiding place and the song is sung again. The familiar finger play may be used as an introduction to this song.

> *Teacher:* Where is _____(name)_____ ?
> Where is _____(name)_____ ?
> *Child:* Here I am. Here I am.
> *Teacher:* How are you this morning?
> *Child:* Very well, I thank you!

Teacher: Run away, run away.
Finale: Where is everybody?
  Where is everybody?
Children: Here we are. Here we are.
Teacher: How are you this morning?
Children: Very well, we thank you.
Teacher: Run away, run away.

Move and Freeze
Formation: Scattered

Children perform a locomotor activity within a designated area and stop on a predetermined signal.

> You may walk in any way you choose within this circle. Try to move without touching anyone else. When you hear the music, stop and freeze in your position. Ready, go!

> *Variations:* Perform the activity with various types of music, to indicate skipping, hopping, jumping, and so on. Change the size of the space within which the children may move. Change directions—move forwards, backwards, or sideways.

Wheels on the Bus
Formation: Seated
Tune: Traditional German folk song

Children act out this song as they sing. They enjoy making up their own lines for new verses.

> The wheels on the bus go round, round, round
> Round, round, round; round, round, round
> The wheels on the bus go round, round, round
> Over the ci-ty streets.
>
> *Variations:*
> The people on the bus go up and down...
> The lights on the bus go blink, blink, blink...
> The horn on the bus goes beep, beep, beep...
> The brakes on the bus go screech, screech, screech...
> The money on the bus goes clink, clink, clink...
> The babies on the bus go wah, wah, wah...
> The mothers on the bus go sh-sh-sh...
> The driver on the bus goes "everybody out"...

Jack-in-the-Box
Formation: Scattered

Each person curls up tightly on the floor and sits still or "pops out" as the last line of the verse is spoken. This rhyme may be practiced as a finger play, with thumbs tucked inside the fist to resemble a Jack-in-the-box.

> Jack-in-the-box
> Sit so still
> Won't you come out?
> Yes, I will!

> *Variations:* "No, I'm eating ice cream." "What will you give me if I do?" "I can't. I'm asleep!" Let the children make up their own endings.

Little Tommy Tinker
Formation: Seated in a circle
Tune: "Little Tommy Tinker"

Everyone joins in the song as one person is designated to be "it". The child's name is substituted in the first line and he responds with a cry. Repeat the game to give others a turn.

> Little_____(name)_____
> Sat on a clinker
> And he (she) began to cry
> "Ma-ah! Ma-ah!"
> Poor little innocent guy (girl).

> *Variations:* "Ouch! Ouch!"; "Oh, dear, Oh, dear!"

If You're Happy
Formation: Seated in a circle
Tune: Traditional song

Children enjoy singing this song which emphasizes various body parts and allows for creative expression.

> If you're happy and you know it, clap your hands.
> If you're happy and you know it, clap your hands.
> If you're happy and you know it,
> Then your face will surely show it
> If you're happy and you know it, clap your hands.

Variations: Stomp your feet, nod your head, touch your ears, wave your hand, turn around.

This Is My Body
Formation: Standing in a circle

As the lines are spoken, everyone pats the designated part of his body in rhythm with the words. After each verse, one child points to another part of his body and names it. All join in to repeat that word four times.

> This is my bo-dy (thighs)
> This is me (clap)
> Look at me (chest)
> And tell me what you see!
>   (child points to part of his body)

Examples: ears, ears, ears, ears; or el-bow, el-bow, el-bow, el-bow.

Show Us What to Do
Formation: Standing in a circle
Tune: "London Bridge"

Everyone joins hands and walks around in a circle while one person stands in the middle. At the end of the verse, "it" demonstrates a body movement which all the children imitate. "It" then chooses another person to take his place, and the game is repeated.

> _____(name)_____ show us what to do,
> What to do, what to do,
> _____(name)_____ show us what to do,
> Show us what to do.

The Fall Season:
A Time of Change

Activities in this chapter focus upon natural changes of the fall season. Emphasis is placed upon a coordinated unit of study wherein the movement-sensory approach facilitates learning for exceptional students.

The teacher is encouraged to utilize audiovisual materials for illustration and, where possible, to involve children in actual observation of nature. It is more desirable, for example, to take the class on a walk through autumn leaves than to view the scene in a movie. When suitable experiences are not available, then it will be necessary to expand sensory awareness through the media.

Once a group has been introduced to the concept of fall, it can begin to transfer information into creative movement. The instructor may prefer to discuss one element at a time, such as fall leaves, and correlate book activities with supplementary materials. For instance, the study of fall could begin with a group event, such as a walk or a film, during which children observe the colors, shapes, and movements of different leaves. After this introduction, the students verbalize their findings and proceed into the exercise "What is Fall?" At this point, assimilation of information and creative expression merge to lead the way to understanding.

This coordination of movement and knowledge allows the special child to internalize learning concepts. His recall of material is also likely to be enhanced through the process of personal involvement.

THE FALL SEASON / 13

What is Fall?
Formation: Scattered

Children stand tall and straight with their arms outstretched, moving only those parts of their bodies indicated by the dialogue.

> Let's pretend that you are a tree. Your feet are the roots, planted firmly in the ground. Your legs and chest form the trunk. Your arms are the branches and your fingers, the leaves of the tree. The trees are standing very tall, because they have been growing for many years. Now it is the fall season and the weather is beginning to change. The days are cooler, the wind comes up, and the *branches sway* a little. The *leaves* begin to *rustle* in the breeze and some even drop to the ground.

> What color are your leaves? Are some of your leaves falling? What other things fall from certain kinds of trees? What kind of tree are you? Why do you think we call this season "fall"?

A Falling Leaf
Formation: Scattered

An excellent introduction to this exercise is to have each child hold a leaf by the stem, let it fall, and observe the way it floats to the ground, hardly making a sound. The children then "become" that leaf in this movement activity.

> You're a leaf, hanging on a tree. Along comes a fall breeze and rustles all the leaves, so that some of them fall off the tree and float quietly down-down-down in the air, to rest upon the ground.

> Fall′-ing, fall′-ing, autumn
>   leaves are fall′-ing

> Fall′-ing, fall′-ing, softly
>   to the ground.

> Red leaves, oranges leaves,
>   yellow leaves, brown leaves

> Fall′-ing, fall′-ing, softly
>   to the ground.

Tiptoe Through the Leaves
Formation: Scattered

Children pretend to tiptoe through the fall leaves scattered about the floor. They may kick with their toes as they join in the chant.

>Now the leaves are all over the ground—red leaves, orange leaves, brown leaves, yellow leaves. Let's pretend to tiptoe through the leaves on our way to school. Chant:

>Tip'-toe, tip'-toe
>Make your feet go tip'-toe
>Tip'-toe, tip'-toe
>Through the autumn leaves.

>Now we're on our way home from school. Let's pretend to kick the leaves up into the air, as we say:

>Kick'-ing, kick'-ing
>Make your feet go kick'-ing
>Kick'-ing, kick'-ing
>Through the autumn leaves.

>Variations: Skip'-ping, skip'-ping. Shuf'-fling, shuf'-fling.

Raking the Leaves
Formation: Scattered
Tune: "Mulberry Bush"

Children pretend to rake leaves into a pile in the middle of the floor as they sing this song.

>This is the way we rake the leaves,
>Rake the leaves, rake the leaves,
>This is the way we rake the leaves,
>So early in the morning.

>Red and brown and yellow leaves,
>Yellow leaves, yellow leaves,
>Red and brown and yellow leaves,
>We rake up from the ground.

Squirrels in the Trees
Formation: Scattered

Two-thirds of the children choose partners to be "trees" and face each other holding hands. The remaining third are "squirrels" who scamper about the room and hide in the trees at a given signal.

Let's pretend it is a fine fall day and these children are gray squirrels looking for nuts on the ground. The rest of you will be our trees that sway a little in the wind. As you are moving, say this little poem together. The squirrels can run inside on the very last line:

Gray squirrel, gray squirrel
 on the ground
Gray squirrel, gray squirrel
 look-ing around
Gray squirrel, gray squirrel
 what do you see?
Gray squirrel, gray squirrel
 hide in a tree!

Repeat the verse, so that the squirrels can find new trees. The class can also be divided so that there is one extra squirrel among the trees and all must scurry for a hiding place.

Mr. Squirrel
Formation: Scattered

The children pretend to be gray squirrels as they act out the lines of this verse.

The squirrel jumps
From tree to tree
He hides from you
He hides from me.
He looks and looks
And looks around
And picks up nuts
From off the ground.*

The Birds
Formation: Scattered

In this activity, children imitate birds who fly to warmer climates for the coming winter. They may join in the chant or simply respond to it through movement.

---

*Sylvia Tester, "Mr. Squirrel." Reprinted from *Happy Times with Action Rhymes,* © 1960, David C. Cook, Elgin, Illinois. Used by permission.

Some birds we know must fly to another place to live as the weather becomes cold. During the fall season large flocks of birds fly south together, flapping their wings as they go. Can you be a bird with us?

Fly′-ing, fly′-ing, across the sky
Fly′-ing, fly′-ing, ever so high
Fly′-ing, fly′-ing, where do they go?
Fly′-ing, fly′-ing, away from the snow.
Fly′-ing, fly′-ing, shall we see you again?
Fly′-ing, fly′-ing, yes in the spring.
Flap′, flap′, flap′, flap′.

How Does a Butterfly Grow?
Formation: Scattered

This exercise demonstrates the four stages of growth in the reproduction of a butterfly. The teacher should proceed slowly, making certain that all children recognize the changes which take place.

You are a little egg just laid on the leaf of a mulberry plant by a beautiful butterfly. Curl up very tightly so that you are round and small. One day all the tiny eggs open up and out come some black and yellow caterpillars. Can you lie on your stomach and wiggle like a caterpillar?

Our hungry caterpillars eat and eat until they become very fat and tired. They decide to take a rest so each one climbs out on a leaf of the plant and hangs himself upside down, just like the letter "j"! Let's see if you can do that on the floor.

While the caterpillars sleep, they slowly loose their black and yellow skin. In its place they have been spinning a slender green thread which wraps around their bodies as they curl up tightly inside. Let's see if you can make yourself small inside that new home.

The caterpillars are gradually changing while they rest. They wait and wait until, finally, one day the chrysalis opens up and out comes a beautiful butterfly. He flaps his wings to dry them and then he flies away! Goodby!

Puddle Fun

Formation: Scattered

Children pretend they are stepping in rain puddles as they chant this poem. They may also "play" in the puddles, as suggested.*

> Piddle, paddle, puddle
> Splish, splash, splosh
> Piddle, paddle, puddle
> Mish, mash, mosh.
>
> Can you make a mudpie?
> Can you sail a boat?
> Can you build a castle?
> Can you sink a float?
>
> Can you make chocolate milk?
> Can you spill it on the ground?
> Can you take a nice mudbath?
> Can you make a mud sound?

Fall Weather

Formation: Scattered

It's fun to act out different kinds of weather, especially when the teacher provides accompaniment on her drum.

> It's a bright, sunshiny day and all the children are playing outdoors. They skip and dance in the sun and shadows because they like to be outside while the weather is still nice. Then, they look up at the sky and see some clouds starting to move across the sun. The sky begins to darken and the wind blows their hair. Can you become the wind? (Stretch out your arms and move about the room on your tiptoes.)
>
> The wind rustles the leaves of the trees and sends the squirrels scurrying inside, for they know a storm is coming. Like a flash in the sky, the lightning crackles (children freeze) and the thunder rolls (children twirl). Rain is on its way and soon the drops will be falling. Can you be the raindrops?
>
> It rains for a while and then stops. All that is left are the puddles on the ground.

---

*The reader is referred to the book, *Pete's Puddle* by Joanna Foster (see Bibliography), which offers many ideas on this theme.

Halloween:
Fun and Fantasy

Fantasy is often utilized by children and adults as a means for self-expression. Halloween characterizations are one type of fantasy through which a child can experiment with actions he might otherwise not perform and display emotions he usually keeps inside. The shy girl, for example, who becomes an evil witch may be enjoying a sense of power she rarely experiences, or the boy who uses a ghost costume to scare everyone may be acting out his own fears and discomforts. Thus, the situation is conducive to creative expression and, at the same time, reflective of inner emotions.

When the fantasy is over, children must return to the world of reality. The teacher should recognize the reluctance of some children to terminate their play and be prepared to offer them firm assistance in this direction. An insecure child, for example, can be reassured of his importance as a class member in order to rejoin the group.

Halloween exercises also offer an opportunity to improve self-image. Through simulated play, a child gains information about his body and its range of movements in space. Discoveries can occur while the child is assuming the positions for a floppy scarecrow, a round pumpkin, or a stern goblin. Further refinement and coordination of body parts will be required if the children participate in role dramatization. Practice is essential to those who have experienced difficulty in this area of development.

Props have a special attraction for the unit because they add to the color and excitement of a make-believe world. Hats and masks can be worn at various times, and the group might construct a scarecrow to see how floppy he really is. A Halloween party is always an appropriate way to end the month.

Scary Skeletons
Formation: Scattered
Tune: "Farmer in the Dell"

Children pretend to be skeletons by letting their limbs dangle and singing this song.

> We're scar-y skel-e-tons
> We're scar-y skel-e-tons
> Clickety-clack down our boney backs
> We're scar-y skel-e-tons.

Big Black Bats
Formation: Scattered

Bats are fun to imitate because they fly at night, flapping their wings, and then go to sleep hanging upside down.

> Let's pretend we're big, black bats who have just come out at night to fly around the dark sky. Bats can't see well but have a special way of sensing that tells them where they're going. Can you squint your eyes to look like a bat's? Can you spread your arms to look like his wings? Let's say it together:

Squint, squint, go the bats
Squint, squint, squint.
Flap, flap, go the bats,
Flap, flap, flap.

Bats make a little squeaking sound sometimes. Can you make it?

Squeak, squeak, go the bats
Squeak, squeak, squeak.

Now it is beginning to get light outside and the bats must go home to sleep. Lay down on the floor and pretend to be a bat sleeping. He sticks his feet to the ceiling, folds up his wings and soon he's fast asleep.

Sleep, sleep, go the bats
Sleep, sleep, sleep.

The Cat
Formation: Crouched on hands and knees

Children become black cats by acting out the motions of this poem. They might also practice stalking mice, arching their backs, and hissing at each other.

> The black cat yawns,
> Opens her jaws,
> Stretches her legs,
> And shows her claws.
>
> Then she gets up
> And stands on four
> Long stiff legs
> And yawns some more.
>
> She shows her sharp teeth,
> She stretches her lip,
> Her slice of tongue
> Turns up at the tip.
>
> Lifting herself
> On her delicate toes,
> She arches her back
> As high as it goes.
>
> She lets herself down
> With particular care,
> And pads away
> With her tail in the air.*

The Old Scarecrow
Formation: Scattered

The children should practice relaxing different parts of their body before they become scarecrows. The action is similar to that of floppy rag dolls.

> The old scarecrow is such a funny man
> He flops in the wind as hard as he can.
> He flops to the right
> He flops to the left
> He flops back and forth

---

*"The Cat," by Mary Britton Miller, from *Poems for Galloping*, A Little Owl Book, (New York: Holt, Rinehart and Winston, 1963).

Till he's almost out of breath.
His arms swing out, his legs swing, too.
He nods his head in a "How do you do?"
See him flippety-flop
As the wind blows hard
This old scarecrow in our own backyard.*

The Goblin
Formation: Standing

This poem has just the right wording for Halloween motions. Let the children stomp their feet on the word "our."

>A goblin lives in *our* house, in *our* house, in *our* house
>A goblin lives in *our* house all the year round.
>He bumps
>And he jumps
>And he thumps
>And he stumps.
>He knocks
>And he rocks
>And he rattles at the locks.
>A goblin lives in *our* house, in *our* house, in *our* house
>A goblin lives in *our* house all the year round.†

Ten Little Pumpkins
Formation: Line

Children may practice this verse as a finger play before acting it out. The pumpkins begin in a line and gradually disappear (sit down), one by one. The exercise is also useful for reinforcing math concepts.

>Ten little pumpkins all in a line,
>One became a jack-o-lantern, then there were nine.
>Nine little pumpkins peeking through the gate,
>An old witch took one, then there were eight.
>Eight little pumpkins (there never were eleven)
>A green goblin took one, then there were seven.

---

*Author unknown.
†(*Italics added.*) "The Goblin," from *Picture Rhymes from Foreign Lands* by Rose Fyleman. Copyright 1935, © renewed 1963 by Rose Fyleman. Reprinted by permission of J. B. Lippincott Company, New York, and The Society of Authors, London, as the literary representative of the Estate of Rose Fyleman.

Seven little pumpkins full of jolly tricks,
A white ghost took one, then there were six.
Six little pumpkins, glad to be alive,
A black bat took one, then there were five.
Five little pumpkins by the barn door,
A hoot owl took one, then there were four.
Four little pumpkins, as you can plainly see,
One became a pumpkin pie, then there were three.
Three little pumpkins feeling very blue,
One rolled away, then there were two.
Two little pumpkins alone in the sun,
One said "so long," and then there was one.
One little pumpkin left all alone,
A little boy chose him, then there were none.
Ten little pumpkins in a patch so green,
Made everyone happy on Halloween.*

Halloween Sounds
Formation: Group
Tune: "Ten Little Indians"

Halloween characters and sounds fill this traditional song which has been adapted for fun and fantasy.

One little, two little, three little witches,
Four little, five little, six little witches,
Seven little, eight little, nine little witches,
They go swish-swish-swish.

Variations:
One little, two little, three little
 tomcats ... they go meow! meow! meow!
One little, two little, three little
 pumpkins ... they go hee! hee! hee!
One little, two little, three little
 hoot owls ... they go hoot! hoot! hoot!
One little, two little, three little
 skeletons ... they go clack! clack! clack!
One little, two little, three little
 black bats ... they go flap! flap! flap!
One little, two little, three little
 goblins ... they go thump! thump! thump!
One little, two little, three little
 children ... they go trick or treat!

---

*Author unknown.

A Witch Hunt
Formation: Seated together

This activity is similar to a "Lion Hunt" in which the group participates in a call-response dialogue with the teacher. Interspersed between the choral parts are various monologues upon which the leader should elaborate. The group may follow by using appropriate motions and sounds to indicate the action.

Let's go on a witch hunt! You repeat each line after me! (Chorus)

We're go-ing on a witch hunt.
We're not afraid.
Of goblins—
Or ghosts—
Or very, very, scary witches!

Here we go through the dark streets and up the hill to the haunted house (slap knees to simulate walking). It's dark out here and scary too! Do you see any goblins? (Shake heads "No.") Do you see any ghosts? (No.) Do you see any witches? (No.) Let's open the door and go inside the house. Cr-e-e-ak! Tiptoe inside quietly. Say, what are we looking for? (Response: "Witches.") Oh!

The leader repeats the chorus and returns to it at intervals during the following events in his monologue:

- A spiderweb brushing against the face
- An owl hooting
- A candle flickering in the dark
- A broom swishing upstairs
- A strange sound thumping
- A door slamming
- The stairs squeaking
- The wind blowing

Final dialogue: Do you see any goblins? (No.) Do you see any ghosts? (No.) Do you see any witches? (Yes! Eek!) Hurry! Back through the wind. Back down the stairs, cre-e-ak. Back past the sound of the door and the thumping! Away from the broom! Away from the candle! Away from the owl! Run till you get home! We made it! Thank goodness!

A Costume Party
Formation: Standing in a circle

A Halloween party is just the right time for children to dress up in costumes. Boys and girls take turns acting out their parts or dancing to music for various themes.

> We're having a costume party and everyone is invited. We'll march around in a circle to display our outfits and hats and then take turns dancing to the music. What do you have on? What character would you like to be?
> It's the girls' turn to be beautiful ballerinas dancing on their tiptoes. Now, the boys can be spacemen walking in their heavy clothes.

Variations: Girls are witches riding on broomsticks.
Boys are cowboys riding on horses.
Boys and girls become skeletons.
Girls are ghosts floating through the air.
Boys are goblins thumping in the dark.

All join in together for a final march around the room and pretend to be whatever they choose.

Growth of a Pumpkin
Formation: Scattered

Children act out the different stages of development involved in the growth of a pumpkin. Pictures help to clarify the transformation which takes place.

> Let's all curl up like tiny little pumpkin seeds that are planted in the ground. I'll check each one of the seeds to see that they are firmly planted. Now, the seeds sit and sit in the ground, soaking up the fresh air and sunshine that helps them to grow. Someone also waters them frequently (teacher pretends to do so).
> Slowly, a little green sprout starts to push its way up (hand) until, finally, there is a large pumpkin vine spread out all over the ground (arms and legs).
> One day a yellow flower appears (head) bursting into bloom. In time, it will become a pumpkin. The sturdy vine holds the

flower which gradually begins to change into a small, green pumpkin (hands over head in arch). It grows bigger and bigger until it is a nice large, orange pumpkin.

 A farmer comes along and cuts the pumpkins off the vine and sends them to the market in a truck. The grocer stacks them in a large box so that boys and girls may have them for Halloween.

Thanksgiving:
Past and Present

Children with learning problems often find it difficult to conceptualize the past, particularly when it has no relevance for them. These activities for Thanksgiving are designed to make this historical event more meaningful and to provide children with representative experiences in the life of the Pilgrims and Indians.

Visual aids play an important part in creating the appropriate atmosphere, especially if the class has access to museum displays and relics. Otherwise, the children may design their own scenery and props in order to provide a suitable environment for the unit.

Most children are familiar with the mannerisms of a turkey or an Indian and will be eager to portray them in a story. The more uncommon role is that of the Pilgrims. Teachers should devote attention to these characterizations during the media presentations, so that children develop an agreeable model for imitation. Everyone may then join in a scenario of "The First Thanksgiving" as each contributes his part to the play. The teacher will discover many related themes for elaboration and can incorporate them into a short skit for the viewing audience.

Gobble, Gobble, Gobble
Formation: Scattered

Children repeat this verse as they crouch down low and bend their arms to resemble turkeys.

>Gobble, gobble, gobble, says Mr. Turkey
>Gobble, gobble, gobble, look at me.
>Gobble, gobble, gobble, says Mr. Turkey
>Gobble, gobble, gobble, I'm as proud as can be.
>
>Strut, strut, strut, goes Mr. Turkey
>Strut, strut, strut, look at me.
>Strut, strut, strut, goes Mr. Turkey
>Strut, strut, strut, I'm as happy as can be.
>
>Oh, oh, oh, says Mr. Turkey
>Oh, oh, oh, don't look at me!
>Oh, oh, oh, says Mr. Turkey
>Oh, oh, oh, it's Thanksgiving I see.

Five Fat Turkeys
Formation: Group
Tune: Traditional

This song may be used as a finger play in which all children participate. A small group can then dramatize the words, as participants assume various roles.

>Five fat turkeys are we-e
>We slept all night in the tree-e
>When the cook came around, we couldn't be found
>And that's why we're here you see.

Variation: Change the number of turkeys to another numeral between two and ten.

A Hunting Party
Formation: Group

The children pretend to be Indians who walk quietly through the woods, hunting deer with their bows and arrows. Other habits of the Indians can be included in the dialogue.

We are Indian hunters who are going out to hunt deer for the big Thanksgiving dinner. Walk very quietly through the forest so that you don't scare the animals away. I hear something moving, over there! Is it a deer? I guess not!

Let's go this way. Oh! There's a deer! Be careful! Draw your arrow very slowly and aim just right. Whoosh! Did you get him? Good! We can take him home, for we only need one right now. The Indians never killed more animals than were necessary. Here we go back to the Indian village!

Indians and Trees
Formation: Grouped according to roles

Children take turns acting out this poem that has parts for Indians, trees, and a tepee. Appropriate scenery and props add to the dramatics.

This is the forest of long, long ago.
Here are the trees standing all in a row.
Look very closely, what do you see?
Indians peering out, one, two, three.
How they are hiding, the forest is still.
Ever so quietly, now they are nearing
The tepee that stands on the edge of the clearing.
Here are the trees standing all in a row.
They knew the Indians of long, long ago.*

Brave Little Indian
Formation: Standing together

This narration is similar to the "Witch Hunt" in that children imitate certain movements in the story (indicated by italics). The leader is encouraged to improvise his dialogue.

A long time ago there was a brave little Indian who lived with his mother and father, sisters and brothers in the Indian village. He was always telling his parents and friends, "I'm going *hunting* for a bear." But they never believed him. So finally, one day he *walked* out of the village with his bow and

---

*Author unknown.

arrow in his hand. It wasn't long until he *saw* a rabbit. Was it a bear? (No.)*

The teacher continues with the story in which the brave little Indian had the following adventures:

- *Saw* a deer
- *Jumped* over a ditch
- *Climbed* up a hill
- *Ran* down the other side
- *Paddled* in a canoe
- *Walked* through the forest
- *Climbed* a tree
- *Saw* a bear

Then proceed backwards through the events to get the brave little Indian home. When he finally arrives at the Indian village, his parents and friends say, "Did you see a bear?" and he says, "Ugh!"

Indian Dance
Formation: Circle

Dancing motions can be imitated as children move their heads and feet in rhythm to the beat. Drum accompaniment is especially effective for this activity.

Hah′-yah-yah-yah
Hah′-yah-yah-yah
In′-dian beats his drum.
Hah′-yah-yah-yah
Hah′-yah-yah-yah
Beats his big′ tom-tom.
Waaaaah!

Pumpkin Pie
Formation: Group

Children perform the actions for this story as the teacher improvises her narration.

---

*More ideas on this theme can be found in *The Brave Little Indian* by Bernard and Bill Martin (see Bibliography). The story of the little Indian in the Martins' book is accompanied by appropriate pictures and suggestions for movement.

Today we are going to pretend to bake a pumpkin pie for Thanksgiving. What do you think we will need to make the pie? (Take suggestions.)

Now, we must all get in the car to go to the market for our supplies. (Teacher talks about the trip and makes appropriate motions for steering the car, going up hills, rounding curves and stopping.) We're here! Each one of you can help us remember the ingredients. Let's put the groceries into the cart and pay the cashier. Time to go back home. (Make motions again.)

To prepare the pumpkin, we must first cook it in water. (Pretend to cut it open and take out the seeds.) While it is cooking, we can make the piecrust and mix the rest of the ingredients. Now we can put them all together and slip it in the oven to bake. Um! Can you smell it? Let's peek at it through the glass. Do you think its done? (No.) Wait again. Is it done now? (Yes.) Let it cool. We can cut the pie now. Time to eat!

The First Thanksgiving
Formation: Group

Everyone joins in this dramatization, which can include costumes and props made by the class.

It is the first Thanksgiving in the town of Plymouth, and the women and children are busy preparing food for the feast. Can you help? What are you going to do? Let's put the food here on the table.

The men are out hunting wild turkeys and catching fish from the rivers. Would some of you like to help them?

When the food is all prepared, the Indians and Pilgrims sit down together for a great feast. The Pilgrims bow their heads in prayer and then everyone enjoys the good food. What are you eating? Can you think of some games to play after dinner?

Who is Thankful?
Formation: Circle

This short round should be spoken in a group where everyone has an opportunity to fill in the last word. A discussion should precede the verse so that each child is ready for his turn.

Who is thankful? (Hands open)
We are thankful. (Hands in prayer)
I am thankful for _____.

In a Cabin in the Woods
Formation: Seated in a circle
Tune: Traditional camp song

Children act out this song using suitable hand motions for the italicized words. After the first chorus, the song is repeated with a gesture taking the place of the first italicized word (for example, draw a cabin in the air). In each verse, another word is left out until all ten are omitted.

In a *cabin* in the woods
Little *man* by a window stood
Saw a rabbit (turkey) *hopping* by
Knocking at my door.
Help me! *Help* me! Let me in!
Or the hunter *shoot* me dead!
I am filled with *dread!*
Little rabbit *come inside*
Safely you'll *abide.*

Christmas and Hanukkah:
Celebrating Together

The holiday season is one of the most vibrant times of year for children as they anticipate the fun and surprises of exchanging gifts. The games and activities in this chapter are intended to capitalize upon the children's excitement and provide a suitable means for expressing their exhuberance.

By participating in movement exercises for Christmas and Hanukkah, children come to recognize differences in religious belief and accept mutual themes of celebration. Integration of spiritual materials will depend upon school regulations as well as the teacher's attitude toward religious matter. In general, a feeling of joy in the act of giving and warmth through friendship are acceptable values to all concerned.

The fantasy of Rudolph the reindeer offers a neutral figure with which all children can identify. Perhaps he is of particular concern to exceptional children, because they empathize with his feelings of rejection by the group. His story is reassuring in that Rudolph gains respect, despite his differences, and proves to be helpful on Christmas Eve.

Several of the following exercises provide an excellent opportunity for dramatization and can be effectively incorporated into a school program. The parts are easy to learn, and yet they provide the special child with an important role in the holiday festivities.

Christmas is Coming
Formation: Seated in a circle

Children chant this old poem as they pass a penny around the circle. Each time the verse ends, the child holding the penny must go to the middle of the group. The verse is repeated several times.

> Christmas is coming
> The geese are getting fat
> Please to put a penny
> In an old man's hat.
> If you haven't got a penny
> A ha'penny will do
> If you haven't got a ha' penny, then
> God bless *you*.*

What is Christmas?
Formation: Standing in a circle

This poem contains many of the delights of Christmas which children enjoy. Movement is suitable to the repetition and can be highlighted by appropriate sounds.

> Christmas is ...
> carolers singing, singing, singing
> church bells ringing, ringing, ringing
> snowflakes dropping, dropping, dropping
> popcorn popping, popping, popping.
> mothers sewing, sewing, sewing
> candles glowing, glowing, glowing
> fires burning, burning, burning
> children yearning, yearning, yearning.
> cookies baking, baking, baking
> *What is taking, taking, taking so-o-o-o long?*

Rudolph
Formation: Group

An adaptation of this popular song provides a seasonal item for the holiday program. Selected words are replaced by gestures, one at a time or all together, as the lines are dramatized.

---

*Beggar's rhyme.

Rudolph the red-nosed_____(make horns with fingers)
Had a very shiny_____(touch nose)
And if you ever saw it,
You would even say it_____(spread hands)
All of the other_____(horns)
Used to laugh and call him names:
  ("nah-nah-nah-nah-nah-nah!")
They never let poor Rudolph
Join in any reindeer games.
Then one foggy Christmas Eve,
Santa came to say:
"Rudolph with your_____(touch nose) so bright
Won't you guide my sleigh tonight?"
Then how the_____(horns) loved him
As they shouted out with glee:
  ("Rah-rah-sis-bom-bah, Rudolph!")
Rudolph the red-nosed_____(horns)
You'll go down in his-tor-y.*

Rounding Up the Reindeer
Formation: Group

Story participation is popular with children, and this selection provides ample opportunity to engage in both movement and sound production. The leader may elaborate upon the dialogue, emphasizing selected words with appropriate motions.

> It is getting to be very close to Christmas and Santa realizes that he hasn't yet rounded up his reindeer. So, one night he *pulls* on his big high-top boots, his great fur cap, his white mittens and his overcoat (act out each motion) and goes outside.
> "Watch out for polar bears," says Mrs. Claus, as Santa goes out the door with a *slam*. "Come, Dasher; come, Prancer; come Donner and Vixen," says Santa. But no reindeer come.

The leader continues with the story as Santa:

> ...*walks* through the deep snow
> ...*thunders* over the bridge

---

*Adapted from the lyrics of "Rudolph The Red-Nosed Reindeer" by Johnny Marks, copyrighted © 1949 by St. Nicholas Music Inc., New York, N.Y. Reprinted with permission.

...*puffs* up a hill
...*steps* slower and slower
...*looks* around the forest
...*walks* to the lake
...*slides* on the ice
...*sees* a polar bear." (Go through the motions in reverse until Santa gets home.)

When he is back inside the house, Mrs. Claus says, "I see you found the reindeer." "Oh, no, I found a polar bear," says Santa. "But the reindeer are here. Look out the window," says Mrs. Claus. And there they are!

Santa's Reindeer
Formation: In pairs

Children pretend to be Santa's reindeer, and they prance all around the room in formation. Use a string of crepe paper on each side of the line to help to hold the "sleigh" together.

> Let's pretend we're going to make a sleigh with Santa's eight reindeer. We need four pairs of children to line up behind each other, and someone to be Santa in the back. Is the team ready to go? We can help them prance by saying:

Prancing, prancing, prancing
See the reindeer go
Prancing, prancing, prancing
Over the fields of snow.

Prancing, prancing, prancing
The team is on their way
Prancing, prancing, prancing
To bring us gifts this day.

Open the Box
Formation: Seated in a circle

The group repeats this verse in unison as each person takes a turn opening the box. Inside, they find small gifts or food wrapped in paper.

Open the box!
Open the box!
O-o-o-o-o-o-o-o-o
Open the box!

Pass Around the Package
Formation: Seated in a circle

Everyone helps to pass around an imaginary package and tries to guess what could be inside. The person who starts the package reveals what was "inside" after the round has been completed.

> We are all sitting around the presents and one of you has a special package. (Leader chooses a child.) Would you like to share your package with us? Show us what size it is with your hands. Can you start passing it around the circle? Let everyone have a chance to hold it and guess what's inside. Remember to keep it the same size as you hand it to the next person. What do you think it could be? Now, you can tell us what it was!

Holiday Dance
Formation: Standing in a circle

This song has one verse for Christmas and another for Hanukkah. Children join hands and circle around together as they sing or chant the words.

> Around and around the Christmas tree
> Around and around we go
> Around and around the Christmas tree
> It's Santa time you know.

> Around and around the Menorah
> Around and around we go
> Around and around the Menorah
> It's Hanukkah you know.

Spinning Dreidel
Formation: Scattered

Children become dreidels as they act out the motions suggested by the verse.

> Do you know what a dreidel is? It's like a top that spins 'round and 'round. Each of you can be a top if you put your arms together straight above your head for a handle. Your body is the round part that spins and spins. As I give your

handle a twist, see if you can spin quickly at first and then gradually slow down to a stop.

Dreidels spinning quickly, quickly
Play with me today
Dreidels spinning quickly, quickly
On this holiday.

Dreidels spinning slower, slower
Play with me today
Dreidels spinning slower, slower
On this holiday.

Dreidels quietly resting, resting
No more can they play
Dreidels quietly resting, resting
On this holiday.

Hanukkah Candles
Formation: A line

The group pretends to be Hanukkah candles as the teacher and children speak their parts. This dramatization is also effective for a holiday program.

Let's pretend that each of you is a candle for the Hanukkah season. As I come around to light your wick, raise your arms together above your head to form the flame. Your body can be the candle standing tall and straight.

Hanukkah candles burning so bright
Hanukkah candles light up the night.

Child responds:

Hanukkah candles flicker and glow
Hanukkah candles bring love I know.

The Winter Season:
Snow Play and Seclusion

With another seasonal change, movement lessons again focus upon the natural environment and related play activities. Though all children may not enjoy the advantages of snow, everyone can join in the fun of pretending.

Imagination exists in every child, but some children are freer with their expression of it than others. These winter activities are designed to stimulate self-expression in the hesitant child by helping him to enact a variety of snow scenes. With encouragement and support he, too, can become uninhibited in his movement and free to interpret themes on his own. The self-assurance one requires can be gained through successful movement experiences.

Later exercises relate to the winter habits of animals and the appearance of plant life. Material should be compared to that of the fall, so that children recognize the significant changes which have taken place. Pictures can be especially helpful in this instance to illustrate the loss of leaves on a tree or the winter retreats of small animals. It is preferable to observe animate objects in their natural setting in order to form a proper frame of reference. Otherwise, the teacher should continually reinforce this information through other media so that children become aware of the cycle of the seasons. This ordering of life can be especially reassuring to those who interpret the environment as a chaotic, disorganized place in which to live.

THE WINTER SEASON / 39

Snow Fun
Formation: Scattered

Snow activities are the subject of this narration which calls for imaginative interpretation by the group.

> Can you act as if you are getting dressed for the snow? What kind of clothes do you need? First, put on your boots—pull hard! One foot and then the other. Now, your overcoat. Be sure to button it all the way up. How about a scarf around your neck? Wrap it tightly! Next, a hat on your head and, finally, some gloves to keep your hands warm. There!
> Let's go for a walk in the snow. Swish, swish, swish. I see something sticking out of the snow. What do you think it is? Whack! A stick! We can use it for a snowman. See if you can find some more. Let's make him big and fat! What shall we do for a face? Can you add the eyes, nose, and mouth?
> I can make a snowball to throw. How about a snowball fight? Look out! What else can we do? I'm getting cold! Time to go home!

The Melting Snowman
Formation: Scattered

This exercise correlates very well with "Snow Fun." It can be used in a combined lesson or on a following day.

> You're a snowman! You are standing in the deep, white snow with a big, round belly, twigs for arms, and a funny face. Now the sun comes out and you slowly begin to melt. First, your head droops a little, then your shoulders begin to sag. Your arms drop and your middle starts to melt, so that you become thinner and thinner. You are slowly getting smaller and smaller until there is just a puddle of water on the ground!

Angels in the Snow
Formation: Scattered

Children lie down on the floor and make angel shapes in the imaginary snow. It is helpful to introduce this exercise by making sand impressions or by drawing around a child's body as he assumes various positions.

> We are playing in the snow and each of us finds a nice clean place to lie down. Can you lie on your back and spread out

your arms and legs as far as they will go? Open and close them several times, like a pair of scissors, trying to push the snow away as you do. Now, stand up and look at the picture you made or, look at your neighbor as he moves. Can you visualize an angel spreading her wings?

Shoveling Snow
Formation: Standing in a circle
Tune: "Mulberry Bush"

Real snow necessitates some shoveling and here is one way to introduce the concept to children: sing while you work! Again, sand might be utilized as an introduction or substitute for snow.

> This is the way we shovel the snow
> Shovel the snow, shovel the snow
> This is the way we shovel the snow
> So early in the morning.
>
> Pick it up and toss it aside
> Toss it aside, toss it aside
> Pick it up and toss it aside
> So early in the morning.

Snow is Falling
Formation: A line, with one pair at the end
Tune: "London Bridge"

Children play this game like "London Bridge" by catching a person under the bridge on the last word, "you." "It" stays inside for the second verse of the song and then takes the place of one of the children forming the bridge. The game can be repeated several times.

> Snow is falling on the ground
> On the ground, on the ground
> Snow is falling on the ground
> And it falls on *you!*
>
> Let it snow for I don't care
> I don't care, I don't care
> Let it snow for I don't care
> I'm having too much fun.

Snowflakes
Formation: Scattered

The class can prepare for this dance by tearing up white paper to resemble snowflakes. Children observe the way it falls to the ground and adapt those motions to the dialogue.

> Snowflakes fall′-ing, fall′-ing, fall′-ing
> Snowflakes falling in the air.
> Snowflakes whirl′-ing, whirl′-ing, whirl′-ing
> Snowflakes whirling round and round.
> Snowflakes fall′-ing, fall′-ing, fall′-ing
> Snowflakes falling on the ground.

Skating on a Pond
Formation: Scattered

Children move about the floor in stocking feet as if they were skating on ice. A slick surface helps to make the exercise more authentic.

> It's a cold, wintery day and you're going skating on a frozen pond. Sit down on this log and put your skates on over your socks. Don't forget to tie them up tight! Are you ready to go out on the ice?
>
> Try to skate very slowly at first, until you warm up. Now can you go faster? Try turning around in a circle. Can you skate with a partner? What else can you do on the ice? Did you fall down? Ouch!
>
> Time to go home! It was so much fun, but there's always tomorrow!

Winter Birds
Formation: Scattered

A discussion of birds and their winter practices provides the background for this little dramatization.

> Little Cock Robin peered out of his cabin
> To see the cold winter come in.
> Tit for tat, what matter for that
> He'll hide his head under his wing.*

---

*Traditional nursery rhyme.

Winter Animals
Formation: Small groups

The winter habits of various animals are described in this movement activity. Groups of children may assume certain roles while others follow the teacher in her discourse.

> Let's find out what some of our animal friends are doing on this cold winter's day. As we start our walk through the woods, we notice that most of the trees are covered with snow. Look for a hollow in a tree. Do you see any squirrels? Remember what they did with their nuts in the fall season? How do they keep themselves warm?

The teacher continues with the narration, adding the following discoveries:

- Ground hogs sleeping in the undercover. (They eat lots of food before they go to sleep.)
- Skunks sleeping underground. (They wake up to look for food.)
- Raccoons sleeping in hollow trees. (They wake up too!)
- A lake, where frogs and turtles live in the warm mud at the bottom. (They have stored their food.)
- Bears asleep in a cave. (They look for food at various times.)

It's time to go back home. What animals did you see? What were they doing? Which animal were you?

One Misty, Moisty Morning
Formation: Standing in a circle

The children repeat the poem as a group up to the last three lines. At that point, the children move about the circle saying, "How do you do" and shaking hands with each other.

> One misty, moisty morning,
> When cloudy was the weather,
> I chanced to meet an old man
> Clothed all in leather;
> He began to compliment,
> And I began to grin—
> "How do you do,"
> And "How do you do,"
> And "How do you do" again!*

---
*Mother Goose rhyme.

Three Special Days:
People to Remember

Lincoln's Birthday, Washington's Birthday, and Valentine's Day are the focus of activities for this unit. The patriotic holidays encourage interest in two historical figures, and Valentine's Day reminds us of the value of friendships and a demonstration of affection. The concept of a meaningful past and a thoughtful present form the basis for activities during this time.

Both Lincoln and Washington are dramatic individuals to remember, and it is not uncommon for children to confuse their lives or contributions to America. Movement exercises offer a method for stabilizing information about these men and for reenacting historical events. It is recommended that children be provided with background material on each president in order to highlight their distinctive lives. In this way, they can form an integrated picture of each man's appearance and significance.

Movement events for Valentine's Day are intended to be fun and intriguing. They are similar to experiences in a normal classroom where children must learn to keep a secret and wait for a turn in the group. There is an element of surprise in the games, and everyone shares in the mystery. As each child has a chance to participate, he becomes both the sender and recipient of good wishes.

Jimmy Crack Corn
Formation: Standing in a circle
Tune: "Jimmy Crack Corn"

This song was one of Abraham Lincoln's favorites. Children act out the movements suggested by the words.

> Jimmy Crack Corn and I don't care
> Jimmy Crack Corn and I don't care
> Jimmy Crack Corn and I don't care
> My master's gone away.

> *Variations:*
> Both hands up and I don't care...
> Turn around and I don't care...
> Hands on hips and I don't care...
> Touch your nose and I don't care...
> Clap your hands and I don't care...

Building a Log Cabin
Formation: Group

Some children can play the part of trees while others pretend to cut them down for a log cabin. A picture of Abraham Lincoln's home will help to define the building.

> Let's imagine that these children are a forest of tall trees and the rest of you are settlers. You are making your home in America and need to build a house, a log cabin like Lincoln's. See if you can cut down a tree and roll it to this spot on the ground. Then all the settlers can help to put the house together. Can you notch the corners so that the logs fit together? Who will gather some rocks to build the fireplace? Do you think it is hard work to build a house?

Log Roll
Formation: Scattered

Children lie down on a rug or mat with arms stretched above their heads and legs together, straight and stiff. The body should remain on a horizontal plane as the child pushes with his hips to turn over and over.

Can you roll on the rug like logs rolling down a river? Put your arms out straight above your head and press your palms together. Be sure to keep your legs stiff. Now, try to push yourself over without bending your body. I'll give you a start if you need it. Can you keep rolling? Try to roll in a direct line.

Who Will be My Valentine?
Formation: Standing in a circle
Tune: "London Bridge"

Children hold hands and walk around in a circle, singing this song, as one person ("it") stands in the middle. At the end of the first verse, "it" chooses a partner who stands with him as the group sings the second stanza. The new child becomes "it" for the next round and the game is repeated.

Who will be your val-en-tine, val-en-tine, val-en-tine?
Who will be your val-en-tine on this happy day?

_____(name)_____ will be your val-en-tine, val-en-tine, val-en-tine
_____(name)_____ will be your val-en-tine on this happy day.

Valentine's Day
Formation: Standing in a circle

Children take turns pretending to be the mailman who delivers valentines.

Postman, postman, please be quick
Postman, postman, who will he pick?
Postman, postman, is it for me?
Postman, postman, it's Valentine's you see!

Five Little Valentines
Formation: Line

This verse can be used as a finger play before a group of children act out the lines.

Five little valentines sitting in the sun
Please give me to mother, said number one.
See my paper so shiny and new
Let me be father's, said number two.
With my ribbons, I'm as pretty as can be
Sister would love me, said number three.
Brother has lots, but he'd like some more
Do give me to him, said number four.
We're all as happy as bees in a hive
Let's run and play, said number five.*

Chopping Down the Cherry Tree
Formation: Scattered, with partners

This activity gives the class an opportunity to enact a famous story. Children enjoy exchanging roles for the dramatization.

Choose partners, so that half of you are cherry trees and the other half are George Washington. In one well-known story about George as a boy, it is said he cut down a cherry tree with his little hatchet. When asked by his father what happened, George replied, "I cannot tell a lie. I cut down the tree." What would you have said? Let's see!

Take your imaginary hatchets and chop at the trunk of the tree. If you are pretending to be a tree, remember to fall to the ground after George has finished. I shall be father who comes to ask each of the boys, "What have you done?"

Good George Washington
Formation: Line, marching rhythm

Toy drums, paper hats, streamers and an American flag are appropriate props for this march. Children can imitate a parade in honor of George Washington.

Good′ George′ Wash′-ing-ton, great′ George′ Wash′-ing-ton
Sing a happy song when his birthday comes
Good′ George′ Wash′-ing-ton, great′ George′ Wash′-ing-ton
Sing a happy song to the beat of drums.
Good′ George′ Wash′-ing-ton, great′ George′ Wash′-ing-ton

---

*Author unknown.

Sing a happy song when his birthday's here
Good′ George′ Wash′-ing-ton, great′ George′ Wash′-ing-ton
Sing a happy song with a rousing cheer. Hurrah!*

Meeting the President
Formation: Group

Children act out the part of nobility who lived in the time of George Washington. Some preparation is necessary for enactment of this scenario.

> You are ladies and gentlemen living in the time of George Washington. You have been invited to meet the first president of the United States! Each of you must get dressed in your very best clothes for the special occasion. Can you remember what the people wore in those days? What did they do with their hair? Look in the mirror!
>
> You will need to be especially polite, so let's practice your introductions. Boys bow and girls curtsy.
>
> Here is the reception line where George Washington and Martha will stand to meet each of you. Who would like to play those parts? Are we ready? Remember to say "How do you do!" as you shake hands.

Yankee Doodle
Formation: Scattered
Tune: "Yankee Doodle"

The group pretends to gallop like ponies as they sing this traditional song. Some children might also like to be soldiers in the image of George Washington.

> Yankee doodle came to town
> Upon a little pony,
> He stuck a feather in his hat
> And called it mac-a-ro-ni.
>
> Yan-kee doo-dle, keep it up
> Yan-kee doo-dle dandy
> Mind the music and the step
> And with the girls be hand-y.

---

*Author unknown.

The Spring Season:
A Time of Splendor

Of the four seasons in the year, spring is the one which seems to direct the most attention towards nature and the reproduction of life. Green plants, blooming flowers, and newborn animals all signify the growth of living things. One senses a feeling of peace and harmony within the system. Such motifs can be conveyed to the special child through movement.

Creative expression is a medium for experiencing that which is imminent as well as a way of implying the unspoken word. "Signs of Spring" and "Spring Kites" are exercises which can portray more than a realistic scene. They can also impart a feeling for spring that goes beyond verbal description. The special child should be exposed to both points of view.

Children can appreciate the earthly qualities of springtime in conjunction with the movement program. The class can share their baby animals, observe the growth of a tadpole, and examine seeds for planting. A variety of nature projects can be used with this unit. Few audiovisual aids will be necessary when the natural environment is utilized as a stimulus for learning.

Plant and animal life should again be compared to previous seasons so that children formulate an accurate account of sequential development. For example, a comparison would be appropriate during the exercise "Flowering Trees," because the class would have had prior exposure to fall and snow-covered trees.

Signs of Spring
Formation: Standing together

Here is an excellent opportunity to introduce children to information about the springtime. The teacher may include as much material as she chooses.

> We're going on a spring picnic today. What shall we take to eat? Let's pack our lunches so that we're ready to go. Um! I'm hungry already!
>
> Shall we start by walking through the grassy fields? Remember to look for signs of spring. What colors do you see? Do you smell any flowers? Let's pick some wild flowers to take back home. Put them in your basket.
>
> Let's go down to the lake. What small animals and insects will we see? There's a frog! Look up in the tree! I see a nest. Are there any eggs in it? How many? Here comes the mother bird. We must leave her nest alone. What else should we look for on our walk? Do you think there is a special feeling about spring?

Spring Kites
Formation: Scattered

Children pretend to fly kites and then become those kites drifting through the air.

> It's a windy day—just right for flying a kite! Have you ever tried it? We will all have a chance today as we fly our imaginary kites in the sky. What color is yours? Can it go very high? Let's spread out as we unravel the string. Don't get your kite tangled up with someone else's!
>
> Up they go—way, way up in the sky. Mine is so high I can hardly see it! Do you think it would be fun to be up that high? Let's see!
>
> Now, you're the kite, drifting way far away. Can you float through the air, bobbing up and down on the string? What happens to the kite if the wind dies down? Can you do that?

Spring Showers
Formation: Seated in a circle

These rhymes are repeated by two separate groups, in choral form. The tone should be soft at first, grow stronger and stronger, and then decrease to only a whisper.

> Group 1: April showers bring May flowers.
> Group 2: Spring is showery, flowery, bowery.*

Springtime Animals
Formation: Scattered

Animal walks provide a stimulus for moving in new ways. These suggestions serve as a starting point for individual renditions.

> How many different animals can you imitate today?

Can you be a ...
   duck and waddle (quack, quack)
   bunny and hop (sniff, sniff)
   colt and gallop (whinny, whinny)
   bird and fly (chirp, chirp)
   frog and leap (croak, croak)

The Secret
Formation: Group

Everyone likes to guess what the secret is while listening to this poem. Children can then assume the roles of the tree, the robin, and "I" for dramatization.

> We have a secret, just we three
> The robin and I and the sweet cherry tree.
> The bird told the tree and the tree told me
> And nobody knows it, but just us three.
> But, of course, the robin knows it best
> Because he built the—I shan't tell the rest!
> And laid the four little—something in it
> I'm afraid I shall tell it every minute!

---

*Adapted from Thomas Tusser, *April's Husbandry* (1557), "Sweet April showers/Do spring May flowers."

But, if the tree and the robin don't peep,
I'll try my best the secret to keep.
Though I know when the little birds fly about,
Then the whole secret will be out!*

Little Bird
Formation: Scattered

This poem is a timely follow-up to "Winter Birds," as it reveals new animal habits for the spring. Children might compare the two verses for a difference in orientation.

Once I saw a little bird come
   hop, hop, hop.
So I cried, "Little bird, will
   you stop, stop, stop?"
I was going to the window to say,
   "How do you do?"
But he shook his little tail
   and away he flew.†

Tadpoles to Frogs
Formation: Scattered

The growth process of a frog is reinforced through this movement exercise. Children will understand the concept more clearly if it is discussed and illustrated in the classroom.

You are tiny black eggs which have been laid in the water by a mother frog. You are curled up round and tight until, one day, the eggs open up and out swims a little black tadpole. You have only a head and a tail! You swim around in the water, looking for food, and you eat and eat. After several weeks, you grow two back legs. Your tail is also getting to be shorter. Then, you notice two front legs have been growing. Finally, your tail is all gone and you have become a green frog!

---

*Author unknown.
†Mother Goose rhyme.

Spring Garden
Formation: Standing together
Tune: "Mulberry Bush"

It's fun to make up verses to this song, especially if children have had some gardening experience.

> This is the way we rake the earth,
>   rake the earth, rake the earth
> This is the way we rake the earth
>   so early in the morning.

> *Variations:*
> This is the way we dig the earth ...
> This is the way we plant the seeds ...
> This is the way we water the seeds ...
> This is the way our garden grows ...

Flowering Trees
Formation: Scattered

Children become spring trees just beginning to blossom.

> Each of you is a tree that is ready to blossom for the spring. You no longer have your coat of winter snow. Now, there are tiny buds on your branches that will open up into flowers. Remember that your body is the trunk of the tree, your arms, the branches and your fingers, the small buds. Slowly, the blossoms open up and we sniff the air for their scent. What color are your flowers? What kind of tree are you? Can you sway a little in the spring breeze?

Ring-A-Ring O'Roses
Formation: Standing in a circle

This traditional game is an enjoyable spring activity. Children skip around in a circle until the last word of the poem, which tells them to fall down.

> Ring-a-ring of roses,
> A pocketful of posies.
> Tisha! Tisha!
> We all fall down.*

---

*Mother Goose rhyme.

Easter:
Animals and Amusements

Easter is a natural extension of spring, with its frequent reference to animals and flowers. It is also a time when children may acquire new pets and look forward to the treat of eggs and candy. Such themes have been employed for imitation purposes in order to provide practice in motor dexterity.

Chicks, bunnies, and ducklings are the subjects in the first set of exercises whose focus is on locomotor skills. Children gain practice in movement by assuming the postures and motions of familiar animals. When a child experiments in this way he must deal with problems of coordination and balance. Similarly, "The Egg Roll" requires skills in agility, balance, and spatial awareness. Imitation offers an effective tool for reinforcement of body concepts and motor control.

Raising baby animals at school can make the movement curriculum more meaningful to children and provide a worthwhile learning experience. Certainly, a child is better prepared to imitate animals when he has observed their habits over a period of time. Hence, the materials for this unit should be alive and manageable, if possible!

The next section of Easter fun encourages children to act out special events that might take place outside the school. Hiding Easter eggs, eating candy, and buying new clothes are holiday activities that children can demonstrate with great self-assurance. The following scenes invite them to engage in motions, such as bending and stretching, which are a part of daily exercise. In addition, dramatization prepares a child for the real event and allows him to role-play various responses.

Baby Chick
Formation: Scattered

This verse is not only fun to dramatize, but also thought provoking.

> Peck, peck, peck
> On the warm brown egg.
> Out comes a neck
> Out comes a leg.
> How does a chick
> Who's not been about,
> Discover the trick,
> Of how to get out?*

Five Little Bunnies
Formation: Squatting in a line

This short finger play adapts easily to an Easter skit and can be enhanced with bunny tails and ears. It also reinforces math concepts.

> Five little Easter bunnies sitting on the floor
> One hopped away, then there were four.
> Four little Easter bunnies looking at me
> One hopped away, then there were three.
> Three little Easter bunnies looking at you
> One hopped away, then there were two.
> Two little Easter bunnies sitting in the sun
> One hopped away, then there was one.
> One little Easter bunny sitting all alone
> He hopped away, then there was none.†

Easter Duckling
Formation: Scattered

Children act out the part of a duckling who waddles and quacks across the room.

> I'm an Easter duckling, see me walk along
> Waddle, waddle, waddle, waddle.

---

*"Baby Chick," copyright © 1933, 1938, 1946, 1958 by Aileen Fisher. Reprinted from *Runny Days, Sunny Days* by Aileen Fisher, by permission of Abelard-Schuman Limited, an Intext publisher.
†Author unknown.

I'm an Easter duckling, hear my little song
Quack, quack, quack, quack.

I'm an Easter duckling, see me flap my wings
Flap, flap, flap, flap.

I'm an Easter duckling
I can do lots of things!

The Egg Roll
Formation: Scattered

It's easier to practice motor skills as part of a game. By assuming the role of Easter eggs, children practice an important balance task.

> You are Easter eggs, ready to be dyed different colors. Roll yourself up tightly, so that you form a round shape. I shall touch each of you magically to make your egg just the color you'd like.
>
> Now, we are ready for the egg roll. You must sit up with your legs crossed and then grab each foot with the opposite hand. I'll show you how it should look. Do you feel all wound up? Try to rock back and forth so that you roll from one side to the other. Can you pretend that you are eggs rolling in the grass?

Easter Egg Hunt
Formation: Scattered

It is fun to follow up this activity with a real Easter egg hunt in the classroom.

> We're going on an Easter egg hunt. But first we have to hide the eggs for someone else to find. Do you have a basket of eggs in your hand? What colors are they? Oh, I see some with stripes and glitter and all kinds of designs. Did you paint them? Where are you going to hide them? O.K. Let's go!
>
> Now, it's time to find the eggs that other people hid. Can you look

in some new places and fill your basket?
Remember to look on top of things and
underneath objects. They could be
anywhere! I see some that no one else
has found! How many do you have?
Did everyone find some eggs?

Easter Candy
Formation: Seated in a circle

A box filled with jelly beans or other small Easter candy is needed for this game. It is passed around the circle until the last word of the rhyme is spoken. At that point, the child holding the box gets to take one piece of candy (unless he's already had a turn!). The round is repeated several times for everyone to enjoy.

> Easter candy, it's a treat
> Easter candy, oh so sweet.
> Easter candy, yum, yum, yum
> Easter candy, I want *some*.

Easter Clothes
Formation: Group

Everybody likes to go shopping for new things. Here's a chance for each child to choose what he wants to wear.

> Here we go shopping for a new spring outfit that you can wear in the Easter parade. Let's go in the department store, where we can find everything we need.
> Girls, first. What do you want to buy? Do you know what size you wear? Think about your favorite colors as you're choosing clothes. That's nice! Try it on!
> Boys, next! What shall we buy you today? Do you like that style? Think about matching your shirt and pants. What color shoes would you wear? Do they fit? Pay the cashier for the clothes you want to buy. I like the new things you selected!

Easter Parade
Formation: Marching in a line
Tune: "Battle Hymn of the Republic"

This song is an appropriate follow-up for the Easter clothes episode. Children will enjoy marching to the music as they display their imaginary apparel.

> Let us march along in the
>   Eastertime parade
> Let us march along as we all
>   begin to sing
> We're all dressed up and ready
>   for the coming of the spring
> As we go marching on.

Growth of an Easter Lily
Formation: Scattered

The nature topic of this exercise is well suited to spring. It provides a setting for original creations within a common frame of reference.

> Each of you is a brown bulb ready to be planted in the earth. One day you'll grow up to be an Easter lily! First, I must cover you with plenty of rich soil and then water you carefully. As you get rest, water, and sunshine, your roots are beginning to sprout underground. Slowly, a slender, green shoot starts pushing its way up through the dirt, until it is above ground. This stalk continues to grow taller and taller and then it sprouts a blossom. The blossom opens after several days to form a beautiful Easter lily. Happy Easter mother!

Easter Vacation
Formation: Seated in a circle

Children speak this round together after which one person suggests something to do. Everyone repeats the idea three times and then returns to the chorus. The game continues until all have had a turn to contribute.

Easter vacation—No more school!
Easter vacation—What shall we do?
Easter vacation—Let's go away.
Easter vacation—Seven whole days!

Variations:
to the beach, to the mountains, on a picnic

The Summer Season:
Recreational Pursuits

The last chapter is oriented toward the vacation theme, rather than the nature theme of previous seasons. The primary objective is to acquaint children with a variety of activities that can be pursued in their leisure time. Suggestions provided through movement may offer the initiative that is needed for participation in play outside the home.

Camping can be one of the most rewarding experiences a child encounters during his summer vacation. The first set of exercises deals with this adventure. Dramatization is an excellent way of preparing children for camp and allows them to simulate motor activities such as hiking, fishing, and horseback riding. A day camp at school is another way of introducing this activity.

The final lessons center around summer fun and the alternatives open to children for recreation. "Summer, Summer" is an appropriate conclusion, once the possibilities of play have been discussed. The activity "Fruit Trees" should be related to the seasonal changes that have taken place throughout the year. It offers a culmination of nature study and the beginning of another year.

Camp Fun
Formation: Group

This narrative includes only a few of the activities that might be encountered at camp. The teacher is encouraged to contribute her own ideas as well as the children's to the list.

> I like to go to camp. Do you? What's fun about it? What's scary about it? Let's just pretend today that we are all going to camp together. What would you need to bring with you? Can you pack all the things in a suitcase? Now, we're ready!
> We'll have to take the car. Everybody pile in! It's a long drive, but I like going to the mountains. Do you get carsick?
> Here we are! Let's take a look at the cabins. I'm going to sleep in this cot. Where are you going to put your sleeping bag? We can all stay here. I'm going outside.
> There's so many things to do here: hiking, crafts, swimming, riding. Which one shall we try first? I like to go to the campfire, too. Time for bed. Good night!

The Bear Went Over the Mountain
Formation: Standing together
Tune: "The Bear Went Over the Mountain"

Children move like bears as they sing this traditional camp song. It's exciting to think of other verses on your own.

> The bear went over the mountain,
> The bear went over the mountain,
> The bear went over the mountain,
> To see what he could see.
>   But all that he could see,
>   But all that he could see,
> Was the other side of the mountain,
> The other side of the mountain,
> The other side of the mountain,
> Was all that he could see.

> *Variations:*
> The bear swam over the river ...
> The bear went into the forest ...
> The bear climbed into the treetops ...

Row Your Boat
Formation: Seated with partners
Tune: "Row Your Boat"

This song takes on a new feeling as children pretend to rock together like rowboats. The leader instructs them to stretch arms and legs out straight until they touch their partner. Children then alternate bending and straightening the knees in order to rock back and forth.

> Row, row, row your boat
> Gently down the stream
> Merrily, merrily, merrily, merrily
> Life is but a dream.

Camp Song—Old Texas
Formation: Seated together
Tune: "Old Texas"

Two separate groups of children sing this song in a call-response style. It is a traditional camp tune performed with the echo technique—the first group sings a line and the second group repeats it.

> I'm going to leave
> Old Texas now
> Ain't got no use
> For the long-horned cow.
> I've plowed and fenced
> My cattle range
> And the people here
> Are all so strange.

> I'll take my horse
> I'll take my rope
> And hit the trail
> Upon a lope.
> Say "adios"
> To the Alamo
> And turn my head
> Toward Mexico.

Way Up in the Sky
Formation: Seated in a circle

This poem is often used as a camp song for young children. It is most effective when accompanied by hand movements.

Way up in the sky (hands up)
   the little birds fly
Way down in the nest (hands down)
   the little birds rest.
With a wing on the left (arm bent)
   and a wing on the right (arm bent)
We'll let the little birdies
   sleep all through the night.
Sh-h-h-h! They're sleeping!
   (head on hands, eyes closed)
The bright sun comes up (hands up)
   the dew falls away (simulate drops)
"Good morning! Good morning!" the
   little birds say! (flap arms like wings)

A Day at the Mountains
Formation: Group

Imaginary vacations are always fun, especially when the leader thinks of many additional adventures.

> Let's go to the mountains today for a hike and a picnic. Pack your lunch and bring some water. Will we need anything else? Be sure to wear sturdy shoes and long pants for the walk. The trail is rocky and dusty.
>
> We're off! There's the mountain over there! It looks steep! Do you think you can climb it? Here we go. Puff, puff, puff. It's hot! How about some water? I see a mountain stream over there. Let's see if the water is clean. Yes! That's good! Feels cool!
>
> Onward! Stomp, stomp, stomp. Up to the top. We're almost there. Hurry up! What a view! Let's eat our lunches here and rest for awhile. Yum, yum! What do you have in your bag?
>
> Time to go! We can go faster on the way down. Whew! Can you make it? The bottom, at last!

A Day at the Beach
Formation: Group

Not everyone has the opportunity to go to the beach in the summertime. But this is one trip that everyone can enjoy.

It's a beautiful summer day, and we're going to the beach. What do you want to take with us? Can you help to pack the car? Be sure to bring your towel. Let's get in the car and we'll be on our way.

There it is. Do you see the ocean? I can smell it from here! Take your things and carry them to the beach. Let's put our towels down here. What shall we build in the sand? I can make a castle. Who is going to dig a hole?

Anyone want to look for shells? We can put them in the bucket. I see some over there. Let's look by those rocks. Be careful! Oh, that's a nice one! I'm hungry! What's for lunch?

(Continue to elaborate as desired, with a return trip home.)

Running Through the Sprinklers
Formation: Standing in a circle

Playing with the sprinkler or hose is a common experience to children in the summer time. They can practice getting wet with this short poem.

> Heel and toe, heel and toe
> Heel and toe and over we go.
>
> In and out, in and out
> In and out and all about.
>
> Jump right in, jump right out
> Jump right through the water spout.

Summer, Summer
Formation: Seated in a circle

Everyone joins in on the first verse, after which one person has an opportunity to tell what summer means to him. The round is repeated for each individual in the group.

> Summer, summer, I like summer
> So many things to do.
> Summer, summer, I like summer
> What does it mean to you?

Fruit Trees
Formation: Standing in pairs

Another episode of seasonal change is summarized in this dramatization.

> In the summer many of our trees bear fruit instead of flowers. Can you think of a fruit that grows on a tree? What color is it?
>
> You may become your favorite fruit tree for today. What will you be? You may prefer to be the worker who picks the fruit off the tree. You and your partner decide which role will be played by whom. Later, you may exchange places. I shall be the supervisor who walks through the orchards. Remember to put the fruit in your basket and not in your mouth! Is your basket full yet? Does the fruit look ripe? Have the birds eaten some of it? What kinds of fruit do you like best? Let's all taste a piece now!

Bibliography

Barlin, Anne, and Paul Barlin. *The Art of Learning Through Movement.* Los Angeles: Ward Ritchie Press, 1971.

Cratty, Bryant. *Developmental Sequences of Perceptual-Motor Tasks.* Freeport, N.Y.: Educational Activities, 1967.

Fisher, Aileen. "Baby Chick." *Runny Days, Sunny Days.* New York: Abelard-Schuman, 1953.

Foster, Joanna. *Pete's Puddle.* New York: Harcourt Brace Jovanovich, 1969.

Fyleman, Rose. "The Goblin." *Picture Rhymes from Foreign Lands.* Philadelphia: J. B. Lippincott, 1963.

Hackett, Layne, and Robert Jenson. *A Guide to Movement Exploration.* Palo Alto, Calif.: Peek Publications, 1967.

Jayne, Mary. *Making Music Your Own—K.* Sacramento, Calif.: California State Department of Education, 1967.

Martin, Bernard, and Bill Martin. *The Brave Little Indian.* New York: Holt, Rinehart & Winston, 1951.

McCall, Adeline. *This is Music: For Kindergarten and Nursery School.* Sacramento, Calif.: California State Department of Education, 1968.

Orff, Karl, and G. Keetman. *Music for Children,* Vols. I–V, London: Schott, 1950.

Tester, Sylvia. "Mr. Squirrel." *Science Studies Resource Booklet.* Elgin, Illinois: David Cook, 1965.